Copyright © 1985 Doug Sewell

Published by
Lion Publishing plc
Icknield Way, Tring, Herts, England
ISBN 0 85648 696 5
Albatross Books
PO Box 320, Sutherland, NSW 2232, Australia
ISBN 0 86760 572 3

First edition 1985

Photographs by Doug Sewell

British Library Cataloguing in Publication Data
Sewell, Doug
 A way in the desert.
 1. Asceticism
 I. Title
 248.4'7   BV5031.2
 ISBN 0 85648 696 5

Printed and bound in Italy by
International Publishing Enterprises - Rome

A WAY
IN THE DESERT

DOUG SEWELL

A LION BOOK
Tring · Belleville · Sydney

INTRODUCTION

When we go through life's difficulties, we are not alone. Many before us have suffered the experience of darkness, only to find it the way through to a new light. Many have found the way of the desert a way through to new life and understanding.

This moving, sensitive portrayal in words and pictures of the desert experience shows that it is not a new one. From the prophets of Bible times and the early Christian fathers, down to our present age, many have found a new peace and renewed spirit in the way of the desert.

Doug Sewell is an Australian photographer and traveller who lived with Bedouin wanderers to take the pictures for this book, and to experience at first hand their way of life.

THE EMPTY DESERT

People do not look for tragedy, it comes. Life has a capacity to inflict suffering upon even the well off and secure. Almost everyone passes through some long and seemingly endless period of distress. These have been likened to travelling through a desert; an experience of spiritual and emotional barrenness. These are dry times.

The desert has been home to many people. During their time in these vast, inhospitable lands they have come to see them in a new way. In the Bible, the people of Israel spent a long period in the desert before they were able to enter the promised land. While they were there, they came to know God face to face. The biblical prophets saw the desert as the place where God was able to prepare people for his work, as did Jesus. Many Christians have gone to the desert to seek a life of prayer and simplicity. The Bedouin tribes see the desert as a living place with which they have learned to coexist.

Far from being the end of the world, the desert in history has often been at the crossroads of civilizations. It has been the battleground for many decisive changes in the course of world events. The focus of human achievement has moved with the growth of technology to the city. Yet, in the empty heart of our modern cities there is an urban desert, new in its appearance, but still as barren as the deserts of old. The loneliness and anxiety which are so much a part of modern city life are the experience of the twentieth-century desert.

The desert is the empty human heart crying out for meaning, love and God.

'The central neurosis of our times is emptiness.'
CARL JUNG

'I am going to take her (God's people) into the desert again; there I will win her back with words of love.' HOSEA

PEACE AND DEMOLITION

On the way from Jerusalem to the desert, the road passes near the city of Jericho. Nestled under the shadow of the high mound of earth that was once ancient Jericho lies a graveyard of empty houses. Where children once chased goats down narrow winding lanes and women hung their washing, now a lost sheep cries and a battered door creaks in the howling wind.

In 1967 an army obliterated the life of the village. Caught in the middle of the battlefield, the innocent bystanders were offered no immunity. Bullets and bombs are no discriminators of people.

The Jordan river valley for over 7,000 years has rarely known a time of peace. Successive armies have murdered and pillaged for one reason or another the inhabitants of the area. The cry of generations rises up from its empty doorways and streets.

The desert has now begun its own invasion. Sand piles up high against the shrapnel-blasted walls, and the wind flicks loose stones from the tops of crumbling parapets.

Scrawled in faint crayon on a wall in Arabic is the single word 'Salaam', and in paint above it in Hebrew, 'Shalom'.

Our whole planet is full of violence. We don't have to leave our front door to find it. The human heart is the root of all evil. It is there that the work of peace needs to begin. It is no wonder therefore that the kind of peace that God can offer is said to pass all understanding. Humanly speaking, it is impossible. God's peace is not just the absence of war, but the active reconstruction of human wholeness. In a violent and crumbling world it is a process filled with risk and pain, for a lot of demolition work has to be done first.

'God's kingdom is creation healed.' HANS KUNG

' "I will restore you to health
     and heal your wounds," declares the Lord,
   "because you are called an outcast, the city of
       God for whom no one cares." ' JEREMIAH

SWEPT AWAY

The Sinai Desert contains many wadis. These are dried-up watercourses with steep sides, eaten out by the surge of water that follows a rainstorm. Sometimes as tall as a man, these surges can flow as fast as stampeding horses.

The high cliffs on either side of me almost seemed to touch at the top when I looked up from inside the narrow wadi. The gentle breeze whistled a playful tune as it danced between the crannies in the rock. Enthralled, I was totally oblivious to the danger. The first indication came with the change in the pitch of the wind's song. The whistle became a cry and then increased to a roar. Without warning, a huge gust of wind blasted my face with sand. Darkness came down and blotted out the last few rays of light. Heavy drops of rain began to fall, landing like stones spat out of the sky.

An awful noise shook the whole wadi and the air became charged. Terrified, I wanted to run and hide, but I could hardly see my hands, let alone a safe place. In that frozen moment that felt like an eternity I pictured my life being swept away. Desperately, I flung myself towards the cliff and groped for a handhold. I found a small crevice and wedged my hand in, braced myself, and waited for the surge . . . but it never came.

When tragedy hits, there is rarely any warning. We are suddenly plunged into an unfamiliar situation over which we have no control. Then, in desperation, we cling to any available crevice, no matter how inadequate. The artificial securities of life are often very flimsy. Our existence is more precarious than we like to imagine, and the future is always unknown.

'The moment passed is no longer; the future may
    never be; the present is all of which man is the
    master.' ROUSSEAU

'For who knows what is good for a man's life,
    during the few and meaningless days he
    passes through like a shadow? Who can tell
    him what will happen under the sun after he
    has gone?' ECCLESIASTES

FIRST AND LAST

A solitary clump of spinifex grows on the slope of an enormous dune. It stands isolated with no other life in sight. The lonely blades pose a riddle: is the clump the yield of a single seed borne by the wind across great distances to become the first settler in this hostile spot, or is it the last remnant of a grassy field which once knew greater days but has dwindled with the onslaught of the desert?

There is something in common which is shared by both the first and the last. They both know solitude. We would expect the first settler to have the greater opportunity, because it is the forerunner of others that will follow, but is this really the case? Could not the lone survivor become the beginning of a new generation, and the pioneer merely wither and be consumed by the drifting sand? We do not know, for we are not able to see the beginning or the end.

To stand alone is frightening, but even more daunting is to try to anticipate what may become of our aloneness. When things go wrong there is always the fear that it will get worse. Sometimes it will, and we then reach a point when we feel incapable of going on. We may feel tempted to go back, live in the memories of the past, and abandon the future. If only we could see that in almost everything that has an end, there is also the potential to begin again.

'It is a peculiarity of man that we can only live by
      looking to the future.' VICTOR FRANKL

'The desert and the parched land will be glad;
      the wilderness will rejoice and blossom.'
      ISAIAH

15

APART AND TOGETHER

A Bedouin tribesman told me, 'Go to the desert alone and you will find community. Go to the desert with others, and you will know solitude.' At the time, I did not understand this puzzling statement.

Eating with my fingers out of one bowl shared between five people was fun at first. But after a week, the stories we exchanged around the camp fire got a bit thin, as did the smiles. During the daytime I would wander off on long walks in the desert. The empty spaces respected my desire to be alone.

On one occasion, I was a long way from camp with no possibility of getting back before dark. All I could think of as I quickened my pace was the fire and the idle conversations of the previous night. The others now became important to me when I needed them.

With a long way still to go, I saw in the haze a herd of goats. A dark figure beckoned me and I followed in the direction of a low, wide tent with its sides opened out. Smiles and handshakes with the Arabic word of welcome, 'mâhâbâ', were offered by each member of the family. A sweet black tea was brewed and passed

around in tiny glasses. I knew I was fully accepted when the family photographs came out. Old and stained, I could tell they were treasured possessions as each was examined under a fading torch. After an hour I reluctantly prised myself away and was escorted back into the moonlight.

People yearn for both closeness and separateness. Our desire to have both leaves us in tension. We are walking contradictions, rarely satisfied with ourselves or others. We dream of escape, not realizing that we cannot be complete until we find our missing dimension in the God who made us.

'What makes man a lonely creature is his
　　　Godlikeness. It's the fullness of the Good that
　　　can't get out or can't find its proper
　　　"other place"'. FYNN

'Know that the Lord is God.
　　　It is he who made us and we are his;
we are his people, the sheep of his pasture.' PSALM 100

FAMILIAR LANDMARKS

In the desert, it's not hard to lose the way. The dunes can drift and change shape in a few hours. Familiar territory can quickly become unrecognizable. Footsteps left in the sand are never accurate markers for retracing a journey.

You soon learn which landmarks are reliable. The big and spectacular things are common in the desert, so it is the odd, small things which stand out: a peculiar acacia tree, a black boulder among pink rocks or an old, broken fence. Landmarks need have no particular beauty, but when you are lost and stumble across one that looks familiar it fills you with hope.

In life it is not hard to get lost. We pretend to know the way, but instead wander in circles or follow others when they too are lost. Sometimes we miss seeing the landmarks because we are waiting for something big to happen that will make the direction ahead obvious. But the way is revealed less by the spectacular and impressive than by the lowly and vulnerable. When I have lost hope or joy, I do not look to the world leaders, but to the old hand that holds mine or the understanding smile. In these little things I find a path for my heart.

God rarely shows the way with a loud shout or a bright light. Rather he comes almost unnoticed like a whisper, a promise of hope. The way of God is revealed in a poor, homeless child, a humble servant, and a man who was rejected and made to die the death of a criminal. Was not Jesus all these things?

'God creates out of nothing. Therefore, until a man
    is nothing God can make nothing out of him.'
    MARTIN LUTHER

'Unless you change and become like little children,
    you will never enter the kingdom of heaven.'
    JESUS CHRIST

CANDLE IN THE BLACK NIGHT

When night arrives in the desert, it comes quickly. The stars, though, come slowly, increasing in number and brilliance until they fill the black vault overhead. For centuries, they have been the guides and companions of the night to the desert people known as the Bedouin. But not every night is clear, and when the clouds blank out the stars and the moon the blackness is total. It is impossible to see anything.

On one such night a Bedouin friend called Sleman lit a candle and placed it in the window of our stone hut. I followed his laughter as we stumbled into the blackness for several minutes before stopping. He then asked me if I could find my way back. I instinctively turned around, but Sleman grabbed my shoulders and twisted me further round to my left. My first attempt had been quite wrong, for there in the direction I was now facing, perhaps a hundred metres away, flickered the tiny candle surrounded by an infinity of blackness.

Its light pierced through the darkness. The faint breeze caused the candle to flicker wildly, but each time it would burst back giving out a new radiance. In all that blackness, the tiny glow shone through and proclaimed silently, 'I am the way home.'

People of faith are not immune to doubt, suffering and despair. When our lives are immersed in distress we may feel totally abandoned, even by God. Trapped in a no-man's land, between an unlivable present and an unthinkable future, every moment becomes a living nightmare. Suffering is unbearable when hope is extinguished. Yet even the faintest spark of light in the darkness is enough to rekindle hope. God's light never goes out. It remains when everything else has ceased – a candle flickering in the blackest night showing the way home.

'To live without hope is to cease to live.'
FYODOR DOSTOEVSKY

'Let him who walks in the dark,
     who has no light,
trust in the name of the Lord
     and rely on his God.' ISAIAH

MOON MEETS SUN

I woke early to make sure I would not miss it. I knew it would only last a few minutes and I would probably not have another opportunity. I dressed quickly, grabbed my camera and hurried to the vantage point. I arrived only a minute early. Floating just above the high western cliff that dwarfed the oasis was the full circle of the setting moon, and behind me, bursting over the top of the eastern wall of cliffs was the rising sun. For less than five minutes I saw the two meet face to face. The western cliff began to glow a soft gold as the moon's white disc kissed its rim and then sank slowly behind.

I felt a little like an intruder overlooking the meeting of two lovers. The stillness of the desert, the slow movement of the moon and the soft warmth of the golden cliff each added something to the enchanting scene. Its beauty washed over whatever memories I had of the previous dark night.

The writer of the Psalms captured it when he said, 'Weeping may remain for a night, but rejoicing comes in the morning.' The dawn has always been a symbol of hope for people everywhere. In beauty and love there is a mixture of joy and sadness which when mingled together touch the heart at its deepest point. When beauty and love can be found in the midst of suffering then that suffering is given meaning. Pain and sadness may remain, but so too comes the ability to rejoice . . . to dance with tears in our eyes.

Beauty and love are not possessions to hold on to, but gifts to be touched by. To be touched is to receive hope. The greatest gift is to be touched by the love and beauty of God.

'He who has a why to live can bear with almost
    any how.' NIETZSCHE

'The Lord's compassions never fail.
    They are new every morning . . .' LAMENTATIONS

HEIGHT AND DEPTH

Cradled in a U-shaped valley, the monastery of St. Catherine is overshadowed by the enormous bulk of Mount Sinai. For centuries, people have considered this to be the mountain on which God spoke to Moses. Standing on its summit is like being on the rooftop of the world. Up there, the mountains of the Sinai peninsula roll away like ripples at your feet. And the wind does not blow, it roars.

When Moses asked God what his name was, he replied, 'I am who I am'. On the top of Sinai, this answer makes perfect sense, as all around the world proclaims the majesty of God. Anything less than this self description would have been ridiculous. God is beyond our comprehension and he appears to be unreachable and unknowable . . .

I hid behind a rock as a bitter winter wind howled over the top, tossing the previous night's snow into the crystal clear air. The white, whirling spray glistened as it crossed in front of the sun. I felt a slight rumble under my feet, and turned to see a boulder laden with snow break loose. It rolled half-heartedly at first, then with increasing speed, down the steep slope, bounced on a ledge, broke in half, and plummeted over a cliff into the abyss. I watched its long plunge until it disappeared behind the cliff edge. About ten seconds later I heard a faint thundering noise echo up from the valley below.

. . . And yet, God chose not to remain 'up there'. Instead, he humbled himself by entering the world of men and women to become one of them and to live among them. He did this not only to bring a message of hope, but to become the embodiment of hope itself.

'If Jesus is truly God, everything is clear; if I
    cannot believe this, everything darkens again.'
    CARLO CARRETTO

'For you know the grace of our Lord Jesus Christ,
    that though he was rich, yet for your sakes he
    became poor, so that you through his poverty
    might become rich.' PAUL THE APOSTLE

THE TREE

On my way along a well-used track in the valley I passed an almost limbless, sad looking acacia tree. In shape it resembled a crippled man shaking his fists at heaven. I thought of a man I had known who suffered from an incurable and debilitating disease. He complained that either God did not care or did not exist, for his anguished prayers to be healed had met with no response. Bitterness and cynicism ate away at him and he died inside long before death came to claim his body.

When I returned by way of the tree I stopped, and saw in it someone reaching out for mercy. I remembered hearing the tragic story of an African woman who, deserted by her husband, had to prostitute herself to survive. She was cast out and humiliated by her family. Alone, she brought up her three young children. Her tearful pleadings to be set free from misery seemed to evaporate into nothingness.

I looked beyond the lonely tree to the vast expanse of blue sky. God seemed so remote from human suffering. How could he possibly understand what it would be like to live with constant pain or loneliness?

At dusk, I again passed by the tree and gave it a quick glance. This time, in the soft light, it took on a different character. I stood beneath it and looked up. Now, it resembled the shape of a tall cross, twisted and bent over by time. Then I understood. God did know what it was like to suffer. He feels as we feel and weeps as we weep and smiles as we smile. We are not alone. God is as close as we allow him to be.

'Only a God who suffers can save us.'
DIETRICH BONHOEFFER

'He was pierced for our transgressions,
    he was crushed for our iniquities;
the punishment that brought us peace was upon
    him, and by his wounds we are healed.' ISAIAH

FOOTPRINTS IN SAND

Around the camp fire many stories change hands among the Bedouin. One story I heard was about two desert travellers whose camels had escaped in the night. They were several days journey from water, and agreed to stay together in case of difficulty. Walking only during the cooler hours they searched unsuccessfully for two days. The water ran out and the camels' hoofprints disappeared. On the fourth day, the younger man became delirious, imagining camels in the distance. The next day he lost consciousness. He dreamt that a man bent over him and slowly poured water into his parched throat.

The following morning, while lying half-awake, he saw the two camels chewing a thorn bush. He then remembered his companion whom he could not recollect seeing for days. With the second camel in tow he rode off and retraced his journey by following a single set of footprints. After an hour, he suddenly saw his companion, carrying the water can which looked full.

Over tea the younger man said, 'Why did you leave me when I was ill? Didn't we agree to stay together?'

'I did not leave you,' the other replied.

'But there is only one set of footprints where I came from,' quizzed the first man.

The other smiled. 'Those footprints,' he explained, 'belong to two men. When you collapsed, I carried you on my shoulders to where I found the camels yesterday. Then I found water and last night quenched your thirst. I returned to the spring early this morning and was coming back when you met me.'

When they continued on their return journey, he learnt something more about his companion. All that afternoon and through the next day, he saw the footprints in the sand become those of one person and then two, only to become those of one again, repeated many, many times over.

'We will never really know God as a
        compassionate God if we do not understand
        with our heart and mind that he lives among
        us.' HENRI NOUWEN

'God has said, "Never will I leave you; never will
        I forsake you." ' HEBREWS

DEAD WATER

Some four hundred metres below sea level is a large body of water which has no outlet. Water laden with salts flows in and then stops. Evaporation causes the water level to stay much the same but the mineral content keeps increasing in concentration. Though the water is very deep it is so salty it cannot sustain any life. It has found its place of rest but in turn has become useless. The place is called the Dead Sea.

Without movement, water becomes stagnant. To enable life to exist within its world, it needs to flow. Still water may seem peaceful, but beneath its placid surface a gradual process of decay is taking place.

One of the Desert Fathers, a group of Christians who sought wisdom in the desert, was called Abba John. He prayed that his inner conflict would be taken away from him so that he might become free from care. He went and told an old man, 'I find myself in peace, without an enemy.' The old man said to him 'Go, beseech God to stir up warfare (within you) so that you may regain the affliction and humility that you used to have; for it is by warfare

that the soul makes progress.' So he prayed to God, and when warfare came he no longer prayed that it might be taken away, but said, 'Lord, give me strength for the fight.'

God has placed within the human heart a restlessness that makes it long for wholeness and completeness. The Hebrew word for this is shalom, which is interpreted as peace. Wholeness, though, is not peaceful in a static sense. It comes not from passivity but activity which is in harmony with the activity of God. If life is to be continually renewed it will involve conflict and struggle. God does not offer passive peace, but instead an active hope which calls us forward.

'You have made us for yourself, and our hearts are
    restless till they find their rest in you.' AUGUSTINE

'I am making a way in the desert
    and streams in the wasteland...
    to give drink to my people...' ISAIAH

HOPE AND EXPECTATION

In the middle of the Negev desert lies a beautiful canyon called 'En Mor. It was one place I specially wanted to visit. A morning storm prevented my planned early departure, so it was early afternoon when I finally set off. A rough path guided me at first, but it petered out at the base of a large, rocky hill. I decided to go around the right hand face of the hill. When I rounded it, I could see a pink line just below the horizon. Thinking that this was the canyon, I marched off down the slope.

After walking to where I thought the canyon would be, all I could see stretching to the horizon was flat desert. I must have covered ten kilometres in my two hours of hiking, yet I seemed to be no closer to my objective. There were about two hours of sunlight left, so I decided to go on for another half hour. I was getting annoyed with myself and complained at the horizon for not getting any closer. My deadline passed, but I kept walking for fifteen more minutes. Then I ran the last five minutes, but still saw only flat plain. Dejected, I gave up and started back.

I decided to take a short cut back, straight over the top of the hill. When I reached the summit I looked down the other side, and there, about a kilometre away, was the beginning of the canyon.

Hope and expectation are different. Expectation wants something to happen in a particular way – usually my way. It demands and seeks to possess. It is narrow in its field of vision, like looking down the wrong end of a telescope. Expectations can end up consuming and possessing us. Hope, on the other hand, is open-ended and broad in its vision. It is like looking to the whole horizon – not just to one particular point. It is flexible and willing to change direction. And finally, hope learns to accept obstacles and move around them.

'In this world there are only two tragedies.
One is not getting what one wants, and the
other is getting it.' OSCAR WILDE

'So we fix our eyes not on what is seen, but on
what is unseen. For what is seen is temporary,
but what is unseen is eternal.' PAUL THE APOSTLE

WATER AND STONE

The extraordinary beauty of the 'En Mor Canyon was accentuated by the long shadows of the late afternoon. The colours changed from brilliant gold to pastel pink, and then to a deep purple as they mirrored the sun's fading rays. This wonderful spectacle was more than I had ever expected. The canyon appeared to be endless, reaching as far as I could see. As I stood on the edge of the escarpment with the plain behind me, the panorama evoked unquestionable awe. I felt, like the ancient prophets, that the desert demanded respect. There was nothing insipid about this place or its creator. God, in the desert, asserts his infinite power and man becomes fragile and insignificant.

As I contemplated the view, a drop of rain landed on my head and then another spattered on a rock by my feet. It hit the hard surface and ran off down the slope carrying a few particles of dirt with it. Several more drops fell and then it stopped. Along the floor of the canyon a tiny river meandered between the steep slopes. It was this water which over countless years had carved the ravines

into what was once a flat plain. It was hard to imagine, as the drop that had landed on my head was so soft.

Later, I came across this saying of Abba Poemen, who was a Desert Father: 'The nature of water is soft, that of stone is hard; but if a bottle is hung above the stone, allowing the water to fall drop by drop, it wears away the stone. So it is with the word of God; it is soft and our heart is hard, but the man who hears the word of God often, opens his heart to the fear of God.'

God's great power is only surpassed by his patience and love.

'Jesus is a God whom we can approach without
    pride and before whom we can humble
    ourselves without despair.' BLAISE PASCAL

'I will give you a new heart and put a new spirit in
    you; I will remove from you your heart of
    stone and give you a heart of flesh.' EZEKIEL

WATER FROM SAND

Wadis Wâtir winds its way between high, jagged mountains. We were like ants in a world of giants. After three hours' journey, we stopped our camels and Sleman said he was going to get water. I could not see from where, as we were surrounded by rock and dry sand. He followed a small ravine off to one side of the wadi and knelt beneath a rock overhang. Coming out of a crack in the bottom of the rock was a trickle of water. By scooping out some sand, he formed a small pool from which he filled our can with water. I suggested we might fill a second can, trying to anticipate the long, dry trail ahead of us. 'No', he said, 'we will only take what we need.'

We rested for tea and then I recalled a story which is attributed to Abba Bessarion, another of the Desert Fathers, and I passed it on to Sleman:

'Two men, one the disciple of the other, were walking in the desert beside the sea when the younger man said, "Father, I am very thirsty." The old man said a prayer and then said, "Drink some of the sea water." The water proved sweet when he drank some. He even poured some into a leather bottle for fear of being thirsty later on. Seeing this, the old man asked why he was taking some. The younger man replied, "Forgive me, it is for fear of being thirsty later on." Then the old man said, "God is here, God is everywhere." '

Sleman chuckled and said he would remember the story.

That afternoon, Sleman delighted in stopping almost every hour and showing me each time another hidden spring of water which seemed to trickle out of nowhere. The desert is a dry place, but it is full of water – you only need to know where to look to find it.

'God reveals himself to the little and wounded and
        to each of us to the extent that we accept that
        we are little and wounded.' JEAN VANIER

'Seek first his kingdom and his righteousness,
        and all these things will be given to you as
        well. Therefore do not worry about
        tomorrow, for tomorrow will worry about
        itself.' JESUS CHRIST

OPEN HEARTS AND HANDS

On the coast of the Gulf of Aqaba, the Tarrabeen Bedouin tribe have erected a few huts out of flimsy driftwood, corrugated iron sheets and building materials discarded by the Israelis before they pulled out in 1982. Early each morning, the Bedouin girls bring their sheep and goats to drink at an old well in the courtyard of an Ottoman prison, now in ruins, before taking them out to the distant mountains to graze. The pattern of life for the Bedouin has not changed significantly for centuries. The customs, laws, lifestyle and way of dress are similar to those of the ancient tribes of Israel who lived in the Sinai for forty years during the Exodus from Egypt.

The Bedouin live simply and travel light. Possessions are not important to them, but people are. The large, extended family is the heart of the community, and it is always open to receive strangers. I soon became one of them and as the new arrival I was offered the best that they had. The best sheep was killed for the meal prepared in my honour and I had no choice but to sleep on the only couch while the family slept on the floor. My embarrassed protests made no difference; they insisted and that was that. Hospitality is a way of life extended to all. While materially poor, the Bedouin I met live life to the fullest because their hearts and hands are always open, both to give and receive.

Western people are very much the opposite of the Bedouin. Our laws are often designed to protect property more than people. We are possessed by our possessions and seek to possess others. Ideals can be quickly discarded as impractical, and violence in society becomes a necessary evil. We may be tempted to pride ourselves that we are more advanced than the Bedouin people, but in reality they have a lot to teach us about the true quality of life.

'Much violence is based on the illusion that life is a property to be defended and not a gift to be shared.' HENRI NOUWEN

'What good is it for a man to gain the whole world, yet forfeit his soul?' JESUS CHRIST

CHIMING DISTANCE

I thought I was dreaming for I could hear bells chiming. Getting up, I peered through the shuttered opening in the hut. It was barely dawn. The chiming got louder and I could detect several different notes and a regular low rhythm. I went outside and could see a Bedouin woman walking four donkeys towards me, along the water's edge. Around each donkey's neck was a bell and each bell chimed a different note. The woman, of course, could easily distinguish between the sound of each bell and so knew where each donkey was simply by listening. Should any of the donkeys go astray, even at night, she could tell which one it was, and where to find it.

The people of the Exodus saw themselves as pilgrims in a foreign and unfamiliar land. They were a people on the road and had to rely on God to lead them every step on that road. They did not always follow him and often took the wrong turn, but God

knew them and followed them along the back roads and around the detours. He never abandoned them and was never far away – out of sight maybe, but within chiming distance.

Life is a journey and the road is long. Deserts fall across our road, but if we accept them as being important stages along the way, then we can move on to the land that is promised which we cannot yet see. For some, the road will cross the desert several times. We may be afraid, hurt or alone, or have nothing left to lose, but there will always be hope, because God will never abandon those he knows.

'Once a man is united to God, how could he not live forever?' C.S. LEWIS

'Give thanks...
to him who led his people through the desert,
His love endures for ever.' PSALM 136